This copy of

THE AMAZING FACT-A-DAY
FUN BOOK

belongs to

_____

THE AMAZING FACT-A-DAY
FUN BOOK

Janet Rogers

Illustrated by Mike Roberts

Beaver Books

A Beaver Book
Published by Arrow Books Limited
62–5 Chandos Place, London WC2N 4NW

An imprint of Century Hutchinson Ltd

London Melbourne Sydney Auckland
Johannesburg and agencies throughout the world

First published 1988

Set in Baskerville
by JH Graphics Ltd, Reading

Made and printed in Great Britain
by Anchor Brendon Ltd
Tiptree, Essex

ISBN 0 09 955390 2

Introduction

Here it is, The Amazing Fact-a-Day Fun Book!
It's packed with more than 365 fascinating facts to
make every day of the year a fun one. There are
facts to make you laugh, facts for you to try out for
yourself and facts that you can use to amaze and
astonish your friends! Here are just a few ideas of
what's in store on the following pages:

Did you know that it's easier to smile than frown? Find
out more on 12 March!
*Did you know that the secret ingredient used in some soft
drinks is made of coal?* Check it out on 8 August!
*Did you know that potato crisps were invented by a Red
Indian?* More information on 1 October!
*Did you know that the word 'Sahara' means desert — so
'Sahara desert' actually means 'desert desert'?* If you don't
believe it, turn to 17 June!

And to make sure that this is your very own
personal fact-a-day book, there's room every day
of the year for you to add your own information.
You could use it as a diary and keep a record of
the things you do each day; or you could keep a
note of your appointments, your friends'
birthdays and other vital information; or why not
try to find your *own* amazing facts for every day of
the year?

January

January 1

Happy New Year!
This is a day for New Year's resolutions, but
there's room for fun facts as well. For instance, it
was the day *The Times* newspaper got its name in
1788, as well as the day Great Britain joined the
European Economic Community — the Common
Market — in 1973. Well, *The Times* may have
changed, but the fun facts go rolling along . . .
and you could make a New Year's resolution to
find a fact a day to add to this amazing collection!

My amazing fact _____

_____

_____

January 2

The people who speak the invented language,
Esperanto, hope that one day it will become the
world's common language. In Esperanto, the
word 'esperanto' means 'one who hopes'.

My amazing fact _____

_____

_____

January 3

Amazing Animals
There is a breed of cat called the Ragdoll. It's a large, long-haired cat with Siamese colouring from America, and it's just as limp as a rag doll.

My amazing fact _____

_____

_____

January 4

January is the month of snow and icicles, snowball fights and sledging — even it it's only on an old tray it's great fun. But did you know that of all the salt mined each year in the world, ten per cent is used to de-ice America's roads?

My amazing fact _____

_____

_____

January 5

January Jape
What do you call a black bird that sits upside down in a tree and screeches?
A raven lunatic!
    That's a joke, but it's a fact that a crow can tell whether or not a human is carrying a gun.

My amazing fact _____

_____

_____

January 6

Medical Madness
Every four weeks we human beings shed a complete layer of skin. It just flakes off, and we never even notice!

My amazing fact _____

_____

_____

January 7

The front door of number ten Downing Street, home of Britain's Prime Ministers, can only be opened from the *inside* — so even the policeman on duty outside has to knock!

My amazing fact _____

_____

_____

January 8

Bodily Business
Going to a party? Just think that you burn up 210 calories (a calorie is food that has been turned into energy) getting dressed, but up to 540 dancing to your favourite pop group.

My amazing fact _____

_____

_____

January 9

If you're not much good at dancing or playing games, here's a fun fact to amaze your friends: get hold of a hard-boiled egg and a couple of raw ones, and ask your friends to spin the raw eggs — they won't be able to, but you will be able to spin the hard-boiled one.

My amazing fact _____

_____

_____

January 10

Men and women who are given the freedom of the City of London have the right to be hanged by a silken rope instead of ordinary hemp.

My amazing fact _____

_____

_____

I THINK THAT'S REALLY INTERESTING, DON'T YOU?

January 11

As a Matter of Fact . . .
The word 'alphabet' comes from the first two
letters of the Greek alphabet, 'alpha' and 'beta'.

My amazing fact _____

_____

_____

January 12

You may be allowed to chew gum in school whilst
peeling onions in cookery class! It is said that
chewing gum whilst peeling onions is a sure way
to prevent yourself from crying.

My amazing fact _____

_____

_____

January 13

What's the best way to catch a lobster?
   No, you don't sit in a lobster pot and make a
noise like a lobster, you soak a brick in paraffin
and put *that* in the lobster pot at the bottom of the
sea.

My amazing fact _____

_____

_____

January 14

Geographical Gem
In Italy, the number 13 is considered *lucky* !

My amazing fact _____

_____

_____

January 15

If you're an avid reader, you might be interested
to know that 57,845 books were published in
Britain in 1986. I'm glad to know that you've
included The Amazing Fact-a-Day Fun Book in
your reading for *this* year.

My amazing fact _____

_____

_____

January 16

An Amazing Anagram
Do you know what word you can get from 'the classrooms' if you jumble up all the letters?

It's 'schoolmasters', and the word that describes the making of one word from another is 'anagram'.

My amazing fact _____

_____

_____

January 17

Happy Birthday to . . .
Muhammad Ali, called Cassius Clay before his conversion to the Muslim faith, and once heavyweight boxing champion of the world. He was born in 1942.

My amazing fact _____

_____

_____

January 18

Are you left handed? In Roman times you'd have been called 'sinister', from the Latin word meaning 'left'.

My amazing fact _____

_____

_____

January 19

Ridiculous but Real
An owl can not only look at objects with both eyes at the same time, but can turn its head in a complete circle. Talk about eyes in the back of your head!

My amazing fact _____

_____

_____

WELL, YOU LEARN SOMETHING EVERY DAY, DON'T YOU...

January 20

Sporting Success
Basketball was invented by accident by a Canadian doctor who was trying to keep his students fit during the winter. He couldn't find any boxes to use as goals and used peach baskets instead!

My amazing fact _____

_____

_____

January 21

When is a dry hole not a dry hole?
    When it is an oil well filled with water — such is the jargon of the oil industry.

My amazing fact _____

_____

_____

January 22

London's population first exceeded one million people in 1811 — and it was the first city in the world to do so.

My amazing fact _____

_____

_____

January 23

Food Fact

In Trinidad a prized delicacy is the tree oyster.
This is an oyster, without a precious pearl, that
actually lives in trees growing in swampy rivers.

My amazing fact _____

_____

_____

January 24

There's gold in them thar hills! On 24th January 1848 gold was discovered in California, and this time the Americans recognized it — nearly 50 years before, gold had been discovered, but nobody knew what it was.

My amazing fact _____

_____

_____

I THINK THAT'S **REALLY** INTERESTING, DON'T YOU?

January 25

Frightening Phobia
If you're frightened of spiders that crawl up the bath plug (or crawl anywhere!) you're an arachnophobic. Don't boast about it though or your friends might go spider hunting to frighten you.

My amazing fact _____

_____

_____

January 26

Many Happy Returns of the Day to . . .
Singer and actress Marti Caine, who was born in
1945. If it's your birthday too, make sure you put
a smile on everyone's face, just like Marti Caine
does.

My amazing fact _____

_____

_____

January 27

What steps would you take if you were being
chased by a tiger?
   Very large ones, I expect, although scientists
estimate that tigers have a success rate of only up
to ten per cent in catching their prey.

My amazing fact _____

_____

_____

January 28

Love thy enemy!
The great white shark has no natural enemies in
the sea — even the killer whales steer well clear!

My amazing fact _____

_____

_____

January 29

And speaking of the sea: when the first-ever nuclear submarine, the US Navy's *Nautilus* set out, it was two years before she returned to her home port for refuelling.

My amazing fact _____

_____

_____

January 30

Superman first appeared in a comic on 30 January 1955, and he's still flying high.

My amazing fact _____

_____

_____

January 31

Fun Fact of the Month
In New York, shop window dummies must wear clothes — it's against the law to let a dummy stand naked in the window.

My amazing fact _____

_____

_____

February

February 1

Food Fact
Milk weighs more than cream, but cream is more fattening because it is richer in fat, and therefore richer in calories.

My amazing fact _____

_____

_____

February 2

Long-distance Laughter
If we could shout loudly enough, and our voices could be carried naturally along the airwaves, it would still take 14 hours for this amazing fact to travel from Australia to the west coast of the United States.

My amazing fact _____

_____

_____

February 3

Geographical Gem
The word 'bungalow' came to the English
language from the Hindi word 'Bangla', meaning
'belonging to the Bengal'.

My amazing fact _____

_____

_____

February 4

Don't try to eat chips near the Baltic Sea, because
it contains the least salt of any sea in the world,
and chips aren't as tasty without salt, are they?

My amazing fact _____

_____

_____

February 5

Did you know that jigsaw puzzles were originally
designed as maps, to help in the teaching of
geography? You do now!

My amazing fact _____

_____

_____

February 6

Long to Reign Over Us
Her Majesty Queen Elizabeth II succeeded to the throne on the death of her father on 6 February 1952.

My amazing fact _____

_____

_____

February 7

Amazing Animals
In Brazil there's a butterfly that looks and smells just like chocolate — how beautifully delicious!

My amazing fact _____

_____

_____

February 8

On this day in 1982, a cat called Pussy gave birth to her 400th kitten.

My amazing fact _____

_____

_____

February 9

Getting snow to melt is a s-l-o-w business, because it takes as much heat to melt a kilo of snow as it takes to boil a litre of soup at room temperature.

My amazing fact _____

_____

_____

February 10

Happy Birthday . . .
Mark Spitz, born in the USA in 1950 and possibly the greatest swimmer of all time. He collected seven gold medals at the Munich Olympics in 1972.

My amazing fact _____

_____

_____

February 11

How did the saxophone get its name?

From the man who invented it, Adolphe Sax, of course.

My amazing fact _____

_____

_____

February 12

Ridiculous but Real

There used to be rubber newspapers for people who enjoyed reading in the bath. Now there's a thought for the Amazing Fact-a-Day Fun Book!

My amazing fact _____

_____

_____

February 13

North and South
North of the equator there are about three and a half times more countries than there are south of the equator.

My amazing fact _____

_____

_____

February 14

St Valentine's Day
No hearts and flowers for the man who gave us all an excuse to be lovingly soppy today — the original St Valentine was actually a Christian martyr who was beheaded in the year 270.

My amazing fact _____

_____

_____

February 15

In 1971 s d vanished today.
    What vanished? I can hear some of you asking.
    Shillings and old pence, Britain's pre-decimal
coins, which now sound as old fashioned as groats
and farthings!

My amazing fact _____

_____

_____

February 16

Success Story
How did denim get its name?
    From the little French town of Nîmes ('de
nîmes' means 'from or of Nîmes', hence 'denim')
This must be the true home of jeans, not the Wild
West, surely?

My amazing fact _____

_____

_____

February 17

Who can jump higher, you or an elephant?
    You can, because elephants can't jump!

My amazing fact _____

_____

_____

February 18

Today is Independence Day for The Gambia, the country in Africa, which ceased being a British colony in 1965.

My amazing fact _____

_____

_____

February 19

Happy Birthday to . . .
Czech-born, Australian-wed Hana Mandlikova, who was born to start blowing hot and cold on the tennis courts of the world in 1962.

My amazing fact _____

_____

_____

February 20

Medical Madness
A Mr and Mrs Ralph Cummins had five children, born between 1952 and 1966. Nothing unusual in that, you might think, except that they were _all_ born on 20 February!

My amazing fact _____

_____

_____

February 21

Pipe of Peace?
Long before the American Indians passed their peace pipe around, they smoked special pipes inserted into their noses —ugh!

My amazing fact _____

_____

_____

February 22

A Name is a Name is a Name
Most Moslem families name at least one child after the prophet, Mohammed, which makes it the most common name in the world.

My amazing fact _____

_____

_____

WELL, YOU LEARN SOMETHING EVERY DAY, DON'T YOU...

February 23

Do you have goldfish? If so, don't keep them in water that's too warm (but don't let it freeze this February, either). Scientists have shown that goldfish remember things better while swimming around in cold water; *what* they remember the goldfish have yet to tell us!

My amazing fact _____

_____

_____

February 24

As a Matter of Fact . . .
The French mean 'pm' when they say 'am',
because 'am' stands for 'après midi', which means
'afternoon'.

My amazing fact _____

_____

_____

February 25

Bodily Business
You would have enough lead to fill about 9000
pencils if you could extract all the carbon from
your body.

My amazing fact _____

_____

_____

February 26

It's hard going being a bee — the 'worker' visits
almost 1500 flowers to fill its honey sac before
flying back to the hive.

My amazing fact _____

_____

_____

February 27

What's a 'fillip'?
    It's what you do when you click your fingers —
and that's a fact!

My amazing fact _____

_____

_____

February 28

Fun Fact of the Month
A state law in Ohio, USA, rules that domestic
animals prowling the streets after lighting-up time
must wear tail lights.

My amazing fact _____

_____

_____

February 29 (Leap Years Only)

Pity St Oswald of Worcester, and anyone else
born on 29 February — imagine only being able
to celebrate once every four years, yet still being
four years older!

My amazing fact _____

_____

_____

March

March 1

There's a saying that March is the month that comes in like a lion and goes out like a lamb, so here's a lion of a fact to start with: lions usually let lionesses attack their prey, then the lions saunter up after the kill and start feasting!

My amazing fact _____

_____

_____

March 2

They're dynamite!
   What are?
   Peanuts: they are actually used in the manufacture of dynamite.

My amazing fact _____

_____

_____

March 3

Hello! Hello!
Today is the day that Alexander Graham Bell was born in 1824. He was the inventor of the telephone, but *he* couldn't ever phone home because both his mother and his wife were deaf.

My amazing fact _____

_____

_____

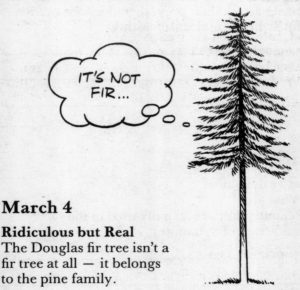

IT'S NOT FIR...

March 4

Ridiculous but Real
The Douglas fir tree isn't a fir tree at all — it belongs to the pine family.

My amazing fact _____

_____

_____

March 5

Tribal totem poles are the Red Indian equivalent of English heraldic crests.

My amazing fact _____

_____

_____

March 6

Clarence Birdseye, the founding father of frozen food, introduced the frozen fishfinger to a supermarket in his home town of Springfield, Massachusetts, USA today in 1930. In Britain, S. W. Smedley of Cambridgeshire started selling sub-zero strawberries in 1936.

My amazing fact _____

_____

_____

March 7

Amazing Animals
A frog's tongue grows from the front of its mouth so that as soon as it turns from a tadpole into a frog it can start feeding itself!

My amazing fact _____

_____

_____

March 8

Many Happy Returns of the Day to . . .
Gyles Brandreth, TV funster and best-selling
children's author. A little-known fact about Gyles
is that he chose his telephone number just to
match the year he was born — and both are
secrets!

My amazing fact _____

_____

_____

March 9

Oh my Word
Guess which word appears most in the Bible? It's
'and', which someone counted 46,277 times, *and*
lived to record it.

My amazing fact _____

_____

_____

March 10

Cruft's Dog Show bowed in to London for the first time on this day in 1886 and everyone was wowed by the entries — they were all terriers.

My amazing fact _____

_____

_____

March 11

Sporting Success
Phil Simms, quarterback for the New York Giants, threw a record 25 out of 27 passes successfully in his team's victory over the Denver Broncos in the 1987 Super Bowl.

My amazing fact _____

_____

_____

March 12

Bodily Business
It's a fun fact that it's easier to smile than to frown. Smiling uses 17 muscles, whilst frowning uses 43. Be kind to yourself (and everyone else) and smile.

My amazing fact _____

_____

_____

March 13

Food Fact
Bombay Duck isn't duck at all — the dish is made from dried fish and curry.

My amazing fact _____

_____

_____

March 14

Where's the most unlikely place to see stars?
    Apart from after a bump on the head, you can see stars from the bottom of a well even in daylight.

My amazing fact _____

_____

_____

March 15

The first Skylab astronauts carried travel sickness pills with them; well, they were a long way from home if they suddenly felt poorly.

My amazing fact _____

_____

_____

March 16

Have you ever noticed how flies always seem to buzz around the middle of a room? That may well be because they're breeding, and that's their preferred place!

My amazing fact _____

_____

_____

I'D RATHER NOT KNOW, THANK YOU...

March 17

Medical Madness
More people catch a cold by holding hands than by kissing!

My amazing fact _____

_____

_____

March 18

And if you're unlucky enough to have a March cold, you might like to know that your sneezes can be expelled from your body at the same speed as a hurricane — at 99 miles (160km) per hour.

My amazing fact _____

_____

_____

March 19

Happy Birthday to . . .
Ursula Andress, born in 1936 and beautiful star
of the very first James Bond film, 'Dr No'.

My amazing fact _____

_____

_____

March 20

Stunning Statistic
China is very densely populated, containing
about one quarter of the world's people.

My amazing fact _____

_____

_____

March 21

As a Matter of Fact . . .
The difference between 'bimonthly' and 'biannual'
is vast, and can be confusing. 'Bimonthly' means
something that happens once every two months
(*or*, twice a month), 'biannual' means something
that happens twice a year.

My amazing fact _____

_____

_____

March 22

Can you tell whether cats and dogs are pleased to see you?

Dogs welcome you with a wagging tail, but cats warn you off with the same action.

My amazing fact _____ _____

_____

_____

March 23

Margaret of Anjou, Queen of England, was born today in 1430, and that's a fact. We know she was very fat because the history books say she was one of Henry V's stoutest supporters — and that's a fun fact!

My amazing fact _____

_____

_____

March 24

The word 'biscuit' comes from two French words, 'bis' and 'cuit', meaning 'twice cooked'. Originally, biscuits had to be cooked twice to make them last twice as long.

My amazing fact _____

_____

_____

March 25

Another Amazing Anagram
What word can you get if you jumble up the
letters of 'nine thumps'?

Here's a clue — you *might* get it at home, or at
school, if you misbehave! The answer's
'punishment'.

My amazing fact _____

_____

_____

March 26

The end of March usually sees the beginning of
British Summer Time, and the best way to
remember which way the clocks move is to
remember that they *spring* forward now, and *fall*
back in the autumn.

My amazing fact _____

_____

_____

March 27

Isn't it wonderful that the evenings are lighter and
there's so much more time for playing outdoors.
But while you're out enjoying yourself, think of
the ancient Egyptians. Even with the largest
sundial in the world — the Great Pyramid of

Cheops — how did they ever tell the time in the dark?

My amazing fact _____

_____

_____

March 28

The first London marathon was run on 28 March 1981. A Norwegian and an American crossed the finishing line hand in hand in a remarkable spirit of sporting friendship.

My amazing fact _____

_____

_____

March 29

This day in 1461 saw the bloodiest battle in the Wars of the Roses, as the noble houses of York and Lancaster fought at Towton. There may be rumblings still between the counties, though nothing as brutal as two-thirds of England's aristocracy being killed in one day!

My amazing fact _____

_____

_____

March 30

Take a piece of paper, any shape, any size and
any thickness, and fold it in half. Easy, isn't it!
Now fold it in half six more times. You may think
it's getting more difficult, but it's a fact that it's
impossible to fold it an eighth time!

My amazing fact _____

_____

_____

March 31

Fun Fact of the Month
A great eponymist was born today in 1811.
What's an eponymist? Someone who gives their
name to the language. This is Robert Bunsen's
birthday who popularized the laboratory burner
which bears his name.

My amazing fact _____

_____

_____

April

April 1

Today is the day that all painters must use polka dot paint, schoolchildren must walk backwards to school and, if you telephone the zoo a recorded message will tell you 'Lion's busy'. If you believe that — you've been had! April Fool!

My amazing fact _____

_____

_____

April 2

Holy Smoke!
Did you know that Saints' Days are celebrated on the day the saints _died_, not on the day they were born?

My amazing fact _____

_____

_____

April 3

You've heard of April showers — well, be *very* glad when you huddle out of the rain that you don't live on the Hawaiian island of Kauai, where the Kokee area has 350 days of rain in an average year.

My amazing fact _____

_____

_____

April 4

Men are on average eight per cent bigger than women, but girls don't mind because although they'll grow up smaller, they know they'll grow up smarter!

My amazing fact _____

_____

_____

April 5

Bodily Business
The hair on your head is actually dead — it is in fact the root of the hair, called the follicle, which grows and makes your hair appear longer.

My amazing fact _____

_____

_____

April 6

Frightening Phobia
If it's true that claustrophobics have a fear of being in a confined space (which it is), do clawstrophobic cats have a fear of sharp nails? If so, scientists haven't proved it yet!

My amazing fact _____

_____

_____

April 7

Cuckoo!
Since about the year 700 (*ages* ago!) the first cuckoo of the spring is always supposed to appear on this day in St Brynach, Wales.

My amazing fact _____

_____

_____

April 8

Have you ever noticed that all the continents' names begin and end with the letter 'A', except 'Europe', which begins and ends with 'E'?

My amazing fact _____

_____

_____

YOU WOULDN'T GET ME UP IN ONE OF THOSE THINGS!

April 9

Mammals are most easily described as creatures that suckle their young, and bats are the only mammals that can fly.

My amazing fact _____

_____

_____

April 10

Food Fact
Chop suey was invented by Chinese immigrants in California to satisfy the Americans' tastes in food. The Chinese don't eat it at all.

My amazing fact _____

_____

_____

April 11

Everyone knows that their own fingerprint is unique. But did you know, too, that so is your tongue print? And did you know that you can 'fingerprint' a cow using its nose?

My amazing fact _____

_____

_____

April 12

On 12 April 1961 the Soviet cosmonaut Yuri Gagarin was the first man to be launched into space. In the 1970s there were so many spacecraft flying around in the stratosphere that rumours of astrojams spread like space dust.

My amazing fact _____

_____

_____

I THINK THAT'S **REALLY** INTERESTING, DON'T YOU?

April 13

Can you guess which is the world's most popular hobby?

Well you wouldn't be too unhinged if you guessed stamp collecting.

My amazing fact _____

_____

_____

April 14

Ho-ho Yo-yo
Originally from the Philippines, the yo-yo was once used as a hunting weapon, not a toy. (And, by the way, there's no truth in the tale that a ship carrying a cargo of yo-yos sank twenty-two times in the Atlantic!)

My amazing fact _____

_____

_____

April 15

GOOD NEWS . . . BAD NEWS
Today in 1955 McDonalds served their first 'Big
Mac, french fries and chocolate milk shake'.
Today in 1912 the supposedly indestructible ship
the *Titanic* sank on her maiden voyage after
hitting an iceberg.

My amazing fact _____

_____

_____

April 16

Happy Birthday to . . .
Spike Milligan, who was born in 1918. A 'Goon'
whose fans include the Prince of Wales, he's still
making us laugh on TV and in his books.

My amazing fact _____

_____

_____

April 17

As a Matter of Fact . . .
The tulip flower gets its name from the Turkish
word 'tulband', which means 'turban'.

My amazing fact _____

_____

_____

April 18

Medical Madness
You can have blue blood on one of two
conditions: one is that you're being smothered to
death (Aaarghh!); the other is that you're a
lobster.

My amazing fact _____

_____

_____

April 19

Amazing Animals
A baby kangaroo is only 1 in (2.54cm) long when
it's born, and has to climb all the way to its
mother's pouch before it can begin feeding.

My amazing fact _____

_____

_____

April 20

In France in 1968 lightning killed only the black sheep in a herd — the white sheep weren't hurt. No one wants to be the black sheep of the family. . . .

My amazing fact _____

_____

_____

April 21

The *Domesday Book* mentions more than 13,000 cities and towns which still exist today.

My amazing fact _____

_____

_____

April 22

There are 17 'Ages' leading up to man's first appearance on earth. These range from the Pre-Cambrian, when there was no life, to the Holocene period of today, which in fact started 10,000 years ago.

My amazing fact _____

_____

_____

April 23

Today the English celebrate St George's Day, because the famous dragon-slayer is the country's patron saint.

My amazing fact _____

_____

_____

April 24

Geographical Gem
The Atlantic islands of the Azores are really the tops of mountains under the sea, and belong to the Atlantic Ridge, which is 52,493 ft (16,000m) high.

My amazing fact _____

_____

_____

April 25

Tell-tale Signs
If you want to know how old a fish is, count the rings on its scales. And if you want to know how old a tree is, count the rings on its trunk. You can't, unfortunately, tell how old a telephone is by counting *its* rings!

My amazing fact _____

_____

_____

April 26

The jaguar is probably the smartest of the cat family, because it can catch fish with its paws.

My amazing fact _____

_____

_____

April 27

April Adventure
Thor Heyerdahl's *Kon-Tiki* raft set sail from Peru for the Polynesian islands on 27 April 1947. He proved that such a journey could have been made years before, without the benefit of the motor!

My amazing fact _____

_____

_____

April 28

Ridiculous but Real
Would a wooden crate sink in water?
  If it was made from boxwood it would!

My amazing fact _____

_____

_____

April 29

Many Happy Returns of the Day to . . .
EastEnders star Anita Dobson, born in 1949.

My amazing fact _____

_____

_____

April 30

Fun Fact of the Month
Sticking your tongue out at a guest in Tibet is
usually taken as a mark of respect, not rudeness,
but it might not be a good idea to try it at home!

My amazing fact _____

_____

_____

May

May 1

It's May Day, but do you know how the Mayday distress signal came about?

It is actually a corruption of the French 'm'aidez', which means 'help me!'

My amazing fact _____

_____

_____

May 2

Do you know why surgeons wear masks when they operate?
It's so that if they make a mistake, no one will know who did it!

That's a joke, but it's a fact that the Ancient Egyptians used to cut off the hands of any surgeon whose patient died during an operation!

My amazing fact _____

_____

_____

May 3

Amazing Animals

The frigate bird, so called because it tags along
with ships, cannot swim or land on water, yet its
diet consists entirely of fish.

My amazing fact _____

_____

_____

WELL, YOU
LEARN SOMETHING
EVERY DAY,
DON'T YOU...

May 4

This day has collected some remarkable facts over
the years. Among them are the fact that Margaret
Thatcher became Britain's, and the Western
world's, first woman prime minister in 1979; the
first Derby race was run at Epsom Downs in 1780;
the world's most famous matador, El Cordobes,
was born in 1936; and the actress Audrey
Hepburn was born in 1929.

My amazing fact _____

_____

_____

May 5

What a Coincidence!
The Dead Sea Scrolls were first deciphered on exactly the same day that Israel was declared a country by the United Nations.

My amazing fact _____
_____

_____

May 6

Sporting Success
The world's first sub-four minute mile was run on this day in 1954 — and success came after a false start! Paced by Christopher Brasher and Christopher Chattaway, Roger Bannister crossed the finishing line first in 3 minutes 59.4 seconds.

My amazing fact _____
_____

_____

May 7

Medical Madness
The Persians used to believe that human tears made excellent medicine for all sorts of illnesses, and used to bottle the tears they shed at funerals.

My amazing fact _____
_____

_____

May 8

Sometimes when you look at lots of weeds, or a huge crop in a field, you might wonder how the earth sustains so many plants. Yet four times as many plants grow in the seas each year as grow on land.

My amazing fact _____

_____

_____

May 9

J. M. Barrie, author of *Peter Pan*, was born on 9 May 1860. In his will, he left all the money earned by his play and book to the Hospital for Sick Children in Great Ormond Street, London, which these days boasts a beautiful mural of scenes from the play.

My amazing fact _____

_____

_____

May 10

Many Happy Returns of the Day to . . .
Writer Richard Adams, author of *Watership Down*, who was born on this day in 1920.

My amazing fact _____

_____

_____

May 11

Tall Stories
Both the Empire State Building in New York and the Japanese volcano Mount Fuji sway in a high wind.

My amazing fact _____

_____

_____

May 12

Probably the most famous nurse in the world was born today in 1920: Florence Nightingale. She was named after the Italian city where she was born.

My amazing fact _____

_____

_____

May 13

Geographical Gem
How famous is Rome?
It must be the megastar of cities, or at least of city names, because there is a city called Rome in every continent.

My amazing fact _____

_____

_____

May 14

Mid-May Merriment
You can't shift a barnacle. Once they're attached to something these sea creatures cling on literally for dear life, and there can be 100 tonnes of barnacles on a single ship's hull.

My amazing fact _____

_____

_____

I THINK THAT'S REALLY INTERESTING, DON'T YOU?

May 15

Head Count
It is estimated that there will be 5,591,828
children between the ages of four and 12 in
Britain by the end of 1988. If they all read the
Amazing Fact-a-Day Fun Book, they'll be the best
informed children in the world!

My amazing fact _____

_____

_____

May 16

A human being has just one heart. A number of
human beings have two hearts because of heart-
transplant operations. An octopus is born with
three hearts.

My amazing fact _____

_____

_____

May 17

On this day in 1890 the first ever children's comic
was produced in America. It was called *Comic
Cuts*.

My amazing fact _____

_____

_____

May 18

Men and boys are more likely to fall out of bed than are women and girls.

My amazing fact _____

_____

_____

May 19

Where did the '?' come from?
Well, it started off when people wrote the letters 'qo' at the end of a sentence to indicate that an answer was needed; 'qo' gradually became 'q̥' which turned into the 'q' without a tail and a full stop!

My amazing fact _____

_____

_____

May 20

The people who discovered the very first fossils believed that the animals they were discovering had all drowned in Noah's flood.

My amazing fact _____

_____

_____

May 21

Ridiculous but Real
Sand is exported to Saudi Arabia from, believe it
or not, Scotland!

My amazing fact _____

_____

_____

May 22

There's no denying it — you're one person in a
million if your IQ (intelligence quotient) exceeds
180.

My amazing fact _____

_____

_____

May 23

Food Fact

We seem to have some fruit and vegetables mixed up: cucumbers and tomatoes (which were once called 'love apples') belong to the *fruit* family; rhubarb is in fact a *vegetable*.

My amazing fact _____

_____

_____

May 24

Have you ever wondered why it's so difficult to swat a fly?

Maybe it's because the eye of the fly has over 4000 facets, or cuts, so that it can see in almost every direction at the same time. That means it sees you coming with the fly swatter!

My amazing fact _____

_____

_____

May 25

Snakes cannot close their eyes. You may think this means they have no eyelids, but you would be wrong. Their eyelids are fused together, and they see through the lower lid which is transparent and completely covers the eye.

My amazing fact _____

_____

_____

May 26

Drip, Drip
You would need 120 drops of liquid to get one teaspoonful — and an awful lot of patience to prove it!

My amazing fact _____

_____

_____

May 27

As a Matter of Fact . . .
One dice doesn't, and can't, exist. The singular of
'dice' is die.

My amazing fact _____

_____

_____

May 28

Sovereign Sailors
King Olav of Norway and King Constantine of
Greece have both won Olympic medals for
sailing.

My amazing fact _____

_____

_____

May 29

Home, Sweet Home
Although the Queen has several residences,
Windsor Castle, where Her Majesty spends
Christmas with her family, is the largest inhabited
castle in the world.

My amazing fact _____

_____

_____

May 30

How high is an elephant's eye?
Of course that depends on how high the elephant is, and measuring that is easy; all you do is measure the distance round one of the elephants feet, and double it.

My amazing fact _____

_____

_____

May 31

Fun Fact of the Month
Many years ago, people used to wear their shoes on either foot, it made no difference.

My amazing fact _____

_____

_____

June

June 1

1 June 1957 saw the drawing of the first premium bond in Britain by Electronic Random Number Indicating Equipment or, as we know it, ERNIE. Have you got a premium bond and the chance to win thousands of pounds?

My amazing fact _____

_____

_____

June 2

June 1953 was chosen for the coronation of Her Majesty Queen Elizabeth II partly because the weather forecasters predicted it would be fine. Guess what? It rained. The coronation was unique, but the weather forecast wasn't!

My amazing fact _____

_____

_____

June 3

However did we manage before the ballpoint pen was invented? It was as recently as 1938 that Hungarian brothers Ladislao and George Biro (yes, really!) put a new kind of pen to paper.

My amazing fact _____

_____

_____

June 4

Food Fact
Peach melba was named after the Australian opera singer, Nellie Melba, whose real name was Helen Mitchell. Peach Mitchell doesn't sound quite so tasty, does it!

My amazing fact _____

_____

_____

WELL, YOU LEARN SOMETHING EVERY DAY, DON'T YOU...

June 5

As a Matter of Fact
'X' denotes a kiss because, in the past, when people who couldn't read or write had to sign documents, they signed with a cross (an 'X') and they also kissed the mark.

My amazing fact _____

_____

_____

June 6

Wild horses wouldn't drag me to Mongolia, in China, where the only true wild horses in the world run free.

My amazing fact _____

_____

_____

June 7

Doorstep deliveries of milk are probably unique to Britain. In the Soviet state of Siberia people usually buy milk the way we buy iced lollies — frozen on a stick!

My amazing fact _____

_____

_____

June 8

Ridiculous but Real
A Gaboon viper snake has been known to stab itself to death with its own poisonous fangs.

My amazing fact _____

_____

_____

June 9

Bodily Business
The funny bone (in your elbow) gets its name from the Latin 'humerus', which is the name of the bone in your elbow. But when you hit your funny bone (and that's not funny!) the pain comes from a nerve and not from the funny bone.

My amazing fact _____

_____

_____

June 10

Happy Birthday to . . .
His Royal Highness Prince Philip, The Duke of Edinburgh, born on 10 June 1921 on the island of Corfu.

My amazing fact _____

_____

_____

June 11

Frightening Phobia
If you're pogonophobic you don't like Billy Connolly, or Rolf Harris, but most women don't scare you at all. Why? Because you're frightened of beards.

My amazing fact _____

_____

_____

June 12

Sporting Success
Rugby union started at Rugby School in 1823
when, during a soccer game, a bright young lad
thought he could score more easily if he picked up
the ball instead of kicking it.

My amazing fact _____

_____

_____

June 13

Unlucky Friday the Thirteenth
If you're superstitious, then you'll be horrified to
know that, over the years, the thirteenth of the
month falls on a Friday more often than on any
other day.

My amazing fact _____

_____

_____

June 14

Horses usually have one bone fewer than human
beings — and yet _we_ ride _them!_

My amazing fact _____

_____

_____

June 15

15 June 2051 is predicted to be the earliest date that people living in London will be able to see a total eclipse of the sun.

My amazing fact _____

_____

_____

June 16

Do you know what a 'palindrome' is?
   A 'palindrome' is a word or phrase which spells the same backwords or forwards. The word 'redivider' is a palindrome, and is the longest one-word palindrome in the English language.

My amazing fact _____

_____

_____

June 17

June Jocularity
The word 'Sahara' actually means 'desert', and the Sahara Desert is roughly the size of Europe.

My amazing fact _____

_____

_____

June 18

Happy Birthday to . . .
Singer Alison Moyet, born on this day in 1961,
who says, 'I'm happiest when I'm miserable!'

My amazing fact _____

_____

_____

June 19

The entire population of the world could stand on
the Isle of Wight — but there wouldn't be room
for anyone to sit down!

My amazing fact _____

_____

_____

June 20

The Black Hole of Calcutta got its name on this day in 1756, when 146 British men and women were locked in a room measuring only 15 × 18 ft (4.5 × 5.4m); only 23 survived to tell the tale.

My amazing fact _____

_____

_____

June 21

Geographical Gem
One sixth of the earth's land is — the Union of Soviet Socialist Republics.

My amazing fact _____

_____

_____

June 22

Only two of the world's mammals lay eggs — the duck-billed platypus and the spiny anteater.

My amazing fact _____

_____

_____

June 23

Eeny, meeny, miny, mo. . . .
Watch out this innocent way of choosing who goes
out is thought to have been used once upon a time
for choosing who went into the sacrificial pot!

My amazing fact _____

_____

_____

June 24

Medical Madness
Molecules of oxygen travel at about the same
speed as a jet plane.
   Breathe in . . . and . . . zoom!

My amazing fact _____

_____

_____

June 25

Mandarin Chinese (or 'guoyu') is spoken by the
largest number of people in the world — 700
million. English comes second, and is spoken by
400 million people throughout the world.

My amazing fact _____

_____

_____

June 26

Did you know that Japanese street corners have
oxygen masks for public use because the volume
of traffic causes such severe air pollution?

My amazing fact _____

_____

_____

June 27

There's survival in simplicity. To prove it, there
are sponges and jellyfish in the seas today in
exactly the same form as there were 500 million
years ago!

My amazing fact _____

_____

_____

June 28

Laughing and crying, though caused by different
feelings, are caused by similar breathing patterns
— deep inhalation and then short, sharp,
exhalation. See if you can recognize this next time
you have a good old laugh, or a good old howl!

My amazing fact _____

_____

_____

June 29

'June' rhymes with 'prune', but can you think of a word that rhymes with 'orange'?

No, you can't, because it's one of the few words in the English language that has no known rhyme.

My amazing fact _____

_____

_____

June 30

Fun Fact of the Month
Gone With the Wind, by Margaret Mitchell, was published today in 1936. The world's best-selling book after the Bible, it's shortly to be displaced from its number two spot by the Amazing Fact-a-Day Fun Book!

My amazing fact _____

_____

_____

July

July 1

School holidays start this month, and a man you've probably never heard of, an Italian called Bernardo Buontalenti, will help you enjoy them.

Why? Because he invented ice cream in Tuscany in the fifteenth century!

My amazing fact _____

_____

_____

July 2

The QE II moves only six inches on one gallon of fuel.

My amazing fact _____

_____

_____

July 3

Antarctica is the coldest place on earth, but its average temperature is still above that of the daytime temperature on Mars.

My amazing fact _____

_____

_____

July 4

It's Independence Day for the United States of America, when all proud Americans will be singing their national anthem, 'God Bless America'.

My amazing fact _____

_____

_____

July 5

The bikini gets its name from the Bikini atoll in the Pacific Ocean, where in 1946 the Americans exploded the world's first atom bomb. This new swimsuit was paraded four days later, on 5 July, at a Paris fashion show and called 'bikini' because it looked like the map of the atoll, pictures of which had been in all the newspapers.

My amazing fact _____

_____

_____

July 6

Bodily Business
At birth a baby has about 350 separate bones.
Many of these join up over the years so that an
adult has 206 bones — give or take a few!

My amazing fact _____

_____

_____

July 7

Did you know that more people drink goats' milk
than cows' milk throughout the world. That's a
fact!

My amazing fact _____

_____

_____

July 8

As a Matter of Fact
The 'Jeep' gets its name from the initials 'GP'. In
the American Army these stood for 'General
Purpose vehicle'.

My amazing fact _____

_____

_____

July 9

What a Mistake!
Marble Arch in London was meant to be the main entrance to Buckingham Palace (which lies to its south-east). But after the amazing Arch was constructed, someone realized that it was too narrow for a stagecoach to go through, so there's never been a grand entrance through it.

My amazing fact _____

_____

_____

WELL, YOU LEARN SOMETHING EVERY DAY, DON'T YOU...

July 10

Geographical Gem
What do Switzerland, Afghanistan, Zaire and Bolivia have in common?

They are just four of the twenty-six countries in the world that have no coastline.

My amazing fact _____

_____

_____

July 11

In 1823 Charles Babbage, a Maths Professor at Cambridge University, designed a mechanical calculating machine which was the forerunner of today's computer.

My amazing fact _____

_____

_____

July 12

Amazing Animals
Rise and shine like an ant!

We know they're very busy creatures, but isn't it amazing that when they wake up they have a good old stretch and yawn — just like humans!

My amazing fact _____

_____

_____

July 13

The letter 'Q' is the least used letter in the English language.

My amazing fact _____

_____

_____

July 14

Today is Bastille Day in France, which celebrates the day in 1789 when thousands of ordinary French citizens attacked the infamous prison to release everyone inside. That's a fact — what's amazing is that there were only _seven_ people inside the Bastille prison, which had a reputation as a very fearsome place.

My amazing fact _____

_____

_____

I THINK THAT'S REALLY INTERESTING, DON'T YOU?

July 15

15 July is St Swithin's Day, and if it rains today legend has it that it will carry on raining for 40 days.

My amazing fact _____

_____

_____

July 16

If a male seal is called a 'bull', and a female seal is called a 'cow', a baby seal must be called . . .
    a 'pup'! And that's a fact.

My amazing fact _____

_____

_____

July 17

Medical Madness.
'Abracadabra!' hasn't always been a magic word
used by conjurors pulling rabbits out of a hat.
Originally it was a word used in a charm for
curing hay fever.

My amazing fact _____

_____

_____

July 18

Have you got a 'sweet tooth'?
  Well, no you haven't. No matter how much you
enjoy sweets, biscuits or cakes, these are all tasted
at the tip of the tongue; taste has nothing to do
with teeth. And another amazing fact is that cats
can't taste sweet things anywhere!

My amazing fact _____

_____

_____

July 19

Lizzie Borden (it is said) took an axe, and gave her father 40 whacks. When she saw what she had done, she gave her mother 41! Lizzie was born on 19 July 1860 and, despite a long trial, was never convicted of murdering her parents. She died in 1927 of old age.

My amazing fact _____

_____

_____

July 20

Ridiculous but Real
The ancient Chinese used to believe that lunar or stellar eclipses were caused by a hungry dragon taking a bite out of the moon or the sun.

My amazing fact _____

_____

_____

July 21

Why couldn't the astronauts land on the moon?
Because it was full!

That was a joke, but back on this day in 1969 it wasn't full, and Neil Armstrong was the first man to set foot on the moon, with the words, 'That's one small step for a man, one giant leap for mankind.'

My amazing fact _____

_____

_____

July 22

Happy Birthday to . . .
TV and stage star Bonnie Langford, who was
only five years old when she first started 'hoofing'
it.

My amazing fact _____

_____

_____

July 23

Food Fact
There is only one food which is naturally blue: the Irish bilberry. Come to think of it, I can't think of a food which is *un*naturally blue — can you?

My amazing fact _____

_____

_____

July 24

Kingly Pursuits
Henry VIII is well remembered for marrying six wives (he did like to chop and change!) and for his musical interest. Less well known is the fact that in his youth he won fame as a hammer thrower.

My amazing fact _____

_____

_____

July 25

The world's first test-tube baby, Louise Brown, was born today in 1978.

My amazing fact _____

_____

_____

July 26

Happy Birthday to . . .
Mick Jagger of Rolling Stones fame, born in
1945, and still gathering no moss.

My amazing fact _____

_____

_____

July 27

If all the people in China jumped off their chairs
at the same time — there would be an enormous
tidal wave in the Western world.

My amazing fact _____

_____

_____

July 28

The New Zealand kiwi is a fascinating bird, with
lots of special features. Here are just two: it can
lay eggs weighing a quarter of its own weight, and
it's the only bird that has nostrils at the end of its
beak.

My amazing fact _____

_____

_____

July 29

Doctor! Doctor!
In England in medieval times, it wouldn't be a doctor you called for if you'd broken any bones, but the blacksmith.

My amazing fact _____

_____

_____

July 30

On 30 July 1966 England won the World Cup at Wembley, beating West Germany 4-2 after extra time.

My amazing fact _____

_____

_____

July 31

Fun Fact of the Month
Do you think the Wembley pitch is big?
    Well, try this for size — it would take 6500 pitches to match the size of the Fort Worth airport in Texas, the larges airport in the world. Things are BIG in Texas!

My amazing fact _____

_____

_____

August

August 1

It's Holiday Time!

If you're going on a package holiday this month, you won't be the first! The first all-in package holiday was from London to Paris in 1861.

My amazing fact _____

_____

_____

August 2

And if you're going to a holiday camp you might like to know that the first holiday camp opened in Caister in Norfolk in 1906.

My amazing fact _____

_____

_____

WELL I NEVER!

August 3

And for caravanners and campers, you might be interested to know that gypsies haven't always lived in caravans; in fact, they used to live in 'bender tents'.

My amazing fact _____

_____

_____

August 4

If you're trying to get a suntan, don't be pig headed — be sensible! Pigs and human beings are the only animals who can get sunburnt, but pigs probably don't know any better, and _you_ do!

My amazing fact _____

_____

_____

August 5

Have you seen the Crown Jewels at the Tower of London?

You wouldn't have been able to during World War II, because they were taken to Aberystwyth in Wales for safe keeping.

My amazing fact _____

_____

_____

August 6

Frightening Phobia
If you absolutely hate going to bed on holiday, try
telling everyone you're suffering from
'Clinophobia'. They'll probably be too amazed to
ask what it means, but it's a fact that it means a
'fear of beds'!

My amazing fact _____

_____

_____

August 7

As a Matter of Fact . . .
The Chinese words 'kung fu', when translated
literally, mean 'leisure time'.

My amazing fact _____

_____

_____

August 8

Would you believe that the sweetening ingredient
in some soft drinks is coal, and that the magic
hardening material in cement is sugar? What a
topsy-turvy world!

My amazing fact _____

_____

_____

August 9

More Irish people live in New York than live in Dublin.

My amazing fact _____

_____

_____

August 10

Geographical Gem

If you get to Canada for your holidays and visit Niagara Falls, take a map with you and go in the summertime.

Why? Because the Falls have moved backwards 7 miles (11km) from where they started, and they've been known to freeze in winter.

My amazing fact _____

_____

_____

August 11

Enid Blyton was born on this day in 1897. She was the author of the Famous Five adventure stories and many other books for children.

My amazing fact _____

_____

_____

August 12

The Glorious Twelfth sees the opening of the British grouse shooting season. It runs until 10 December, and you can only shoot grouse between those dates.

My amazing fact _____

_____

_____

August 13

School Spot
Believe it or not the world 'school' comes from the Greek word for 'leisure'. Don't you just love school?

My amazing fact _____

_____

_____

August 14

August Amazement
Fact for fact, we learn more between our birth and our fifth birthday than we do during the rest of our lives.

My amazing fact _____

_____

_____

August 15

Food Fact
The ostrich lays the largest egg in the world and it would take about 45 minutes to hard boil one.

My amazing fact _____

_____

_____

August 16

Happy 16 August to Liechtenstein, whose National Day it is today. It's the smallest country in the world, and its inhabitants speak German but spend Swiss francs.

My amazing fact _____

_____

_____

August 17

Tea-time

In Siberia until about 100 years ago, blocks of tea were used instead of money. Do you think teabags were the loose change?

My amazing fact _____

_____

_____

August 18

Amazing Animals

When is a dog not a dog?

When it's a prairie dog, because a prairie dog is in fact a rodent.

My amazing fact _____

_____

_____

August 19

Ssh . . .

If the noise and excitement of the holidays are getting the older folks down, here's a fun fact to cheer them up: you can actually buy a silent record on a jukebox.

My amazing fact _____

_____

_____

August 20

Ridiculous but Real
If you're unlucky enough to be caught in a traffic
jam, this fact will drive you ab-so-lute-ly wild.
The Monumental Axis, in Brazil, is the world's
largest road, and there's room for 160 cars to drive
down it side by side!

My amazing fact _____

_____

_____

August 21

Progress means . . . that a manned spacecraft
takes less time to reach the moon than it used to
take a stagecoach to travel the length of England.

My amazing fact _____

_____

_____

August 22

Whatever did we do before 22 August 1932 to
while away the hours? That was the day when
BBC Television made its first broadcast.
Independent commercial television started
broadcasting on 22 September 1955.

My amazing fact _____

_____

_____

August 23

Medical Madness

My face and my . . . were red with embarrassment. Can you guess which other part of you turns red when you blush? You can't? Well, it's your stomach lining, and a *very* clever doctor discovered *that*!

My amazing fact _____

_____

_____

WELL I NEVER!

August 24

Sporting Success

Land ahoy! Captain Matthew Webb was the first person to swim the English Channel from Dover to Cap Griz Nez in France. It took him 21 hours

45 minutes on 24 August 1875 — a far cry from
the latest record of seven hours 40 minutes.

My amazing fact _____

_____

_____

August 25

Do you bite your nails? I hope not!
   But if you really can't resist having a little
nibble, try to leave your thumbnails well alone, as
these take the longest to grow back!

My amazing fact _____

_____

_____

August 26

Why isn't Jamaica growing bananas any longer?
Because they're long enough already.
   That was a joke, now here comes the fun fact —
bananas need people! Left on their own the fruit
would die out, as the trees are not self pollinating.
That means they can't spread pollen to reproduce
themselves.

My amazing fact _____

_____

_____

August 27

Have you ever seen seaweed strewn across a beach?

You'd be amazed at the everyday things seaweed is used for. Apart from making laver bread (a scone made mostly in Wales) seaweed is used in medicine, toothpaste and ice cream!

My amazing fact _____

_____

_____

August 28

And do you think ketchup was invented just to go with your fish and chips or hamburger? Wrong! The fact is that in the last century ketchup was used as a medicine!

My amazing fact _____

_____

_____

August 29

What's the best way to lose weight?

   Be a grandfather clock! Because as it unwinds it becomes lighter.

My amazing fact _____

_____

_____

August 30

Clean that car!
At least, you'd have to keep your car clean in Russia, where driving around in a dirty car is considered a crime.

My amazing fact _____

_____

_____

August 31

Fun Fact of the Month
On 31 August 1968 Gary (now Sir Garfield) Sobers, the Barbadian all-round cricketer, became the first man ever to score six sixes in one over.

My amazing fact _____

_____

_____

September

September 1

Percy Shaw, from Yorkshire, invented cats' eyes in 1933, but *real* cats' eyes glow in the dark because their inner eye has a layer of cells which reflect light.

My amazing fact _____

_____

_____

September 2

Do you like picking blackberries?

They're a wonderful fruit because apart from being delicious to eat, they can be made into wine, used for highlighting your hair, as a medicine for whooping cough or turned into a thirst-quenching drink as soon as you get home from all the picking!

My amazing fact _____

_____

_____

September 3

The game of cricket used to have a poor reputation, and in 1620 Oliver Cromwell was denounced in public for participating.

My amazing fact _____

_____

_____

September 4

Amazing Animals
The tuna fish just keeps moving along — it is never immobile in the water and the fish have been known to swim millions of miles in their lifetimes.

My amazing fact _____

_____

_____

September 5

With all the headgear being worn these days (not to mention the hairstyles!) we are accustomed to weird and wonderful sights. But the first top hat worn in public led to a 50 pound fine for the man who wore it because women were supposedly terrified at the sight!

My amazing fact _____

_____

_____

September 6

'Wonderful! Um, what is it?'

If you've ever had a present you didn't know what to do with, or seen a tool you didn't recognize, you'll sympathize with the person who saw the first screwdriver — which was actually invented before the screw!

My amazing fact _____

_____

_____

September 7

The late General Charles de Gaulle survived 31 assassination attempts while President of the Fifth Republic of France. He died aged 80 in 1970.

My amazing fact _____

_____

_____

September 8

Maurice Ravel, who composed the 'Bolero' music ice-danced by the fabulous Torvill and Dean, also composed piano music to be played by a one-handed man.

My amazing fact _____

_____

_____

September 9

Food Fact
Around the world people eat insects — fried grasshoppers, chocolate-covered locusts, boiled beetles and curried ants — as natually as we drink a pint of milk.

My amazing fact _____

_____

_____

September 10

As a Matter of Fact
The square mile of the City of London does not have a single road. That's not so amazing, though — all the thoroughfares are called streets, as in Aldersgate Street.

My amazing fact _____
_____
_____

September 11

Medical Madness
When maternity wards in hospitals were surveyed for sound the discovery was made that newborn babies cry for 133 minutes each day.

My amazing fact _____
_____
_____

September 12

September Story
How does an elephant hold up his trunk?

Well, he makes no bones about it, because he hasn't got any bones in his trunk — only 40,000 muscles.

My amazing fact _____
_____
_____

September 13

Ridiculous but Real

The Great Dane dog isn't Danish at all but comes from Germany; and of course the Rhodesian Ridgeback (a lion-hunting dog) should now be called the 'Zimbabwean Ridgeback'.

My amazing fact _____

_____

_____

September 14

On 14 September 1752 Britain adopted the Gregorian calendar. This means two things: first, that in 1752 the date went from 2 September to 14 September overnight and there were outraged protests from everyone at the startling loss of 12 whole days; second, leap years fall every four years, except when centenary years are divisible by 400!

My amazing fact _____

_____

_____

September 15

Agatha Christie was born on this day in 1890. She died in 1975 leaving a real-life unsolved mystery as unfathomable as any she had written: she had disappeared in 1926 for several weeks and when she was found in a Yorkshire spa town she offered no explanation.

My amazing fact _____

_____

_____

September 16

Over 4500 singles were released in Britain in 1986, of which fewer than 300 made the charts.

There's an awful lot of unplayed vinyl out there somewhere. . . .

My amazing fact _____

_____

_____

September 17

And by the way, albums were first released on this day in 1933. Only in those days they were called 'long playing 33⅓ revolutions per minute albums'!

My amazing fact _____

_____

_____

September 18

It would take exactly one year to walk the circumference of the earth at a steady walking pace.

My amazing fact _____

_____

_____

September 19

What a Reputation

Two of the world's greatest thinkers — Socrates and Homer — are also considered to have been two of the world's finest writers. But none of their writing is still in existence and their fame is based on other people's commentaries on their work; so you too might be famous one day!

My amazing fact _____

_____

_____

September 20

You may never find a pot of gold at the end of a rainbow, but you can learn a fact about a rainbow — rainbows only occur when the sun is above the horizon at an angle of less than 40 degrees.

My amazing fact _____

_____

_____

September 21

The word 'amen' is common to the Christian, Moslem and Jewish religions, and is surprisingly like the Hindu 'om'.

My amazing fact _____

_____

_____

September 22

Happy Birthday to . . .
Bruce Springsteen, *born in the USA* on 22 September 1949.

My amazing fact _____

_____

_____

September 23

Bodily Business
As awful as it may sound, it is possible for your stomach to burst. It can only hold about 5 pints (2.7 litres), so be careful what you eat and drink!

My amazing fact _____

_____

_____

September 24

If you were born between 24 September and 23 October your sign of the Zodiac is Libra — the scales. And it is the only inanimate sign — all the rest are human or animal.

My amazing fact _____

_____

_____

September 25

Geographical Gem
If you could pour all the world's seas into a pipe approximately 74 miles (120km) in diameter, and 70,000 miles (112,651km) tall, you would reach one third of the way to the moon.

My amazing fact _____

_____

_____

I THINK THAT'S REALLY INTERESTING, DON'T YOU?

September 26

Sporting Success

Ice-skating movements are often named after the people who first performed them, such as the Salchow (after a Swede called Ulrich Salchow) and the Beilmann Spin (after Denise Beilmann of Switzerland).

My amazing fact _____

_____

_____

THIS IS THE BOTTOMLEY BUMP!

September 27

Who'd be a duck when you could be a ship?

The amazing fun fact about these two is that a ship is about five times more efficient than a duck when it comes to converting energy into work.

My amazing fact _____

_____

_____

September 28

Or would you rather be as strong as an ant, and be able to carry 50 times your own weight *and* pull something 300 times your own weight.

My amazing fact _____

_____

_____

September 29

The word 'laser' is actually made of the initial letters of the words which describe what a laser does — *l*ight *a*mplification (by) *s*timulated *e*mission of *r*adiation.

My amazing fact _____

_____

_____

September 30

Happy Birthday to . . .
Ruia Lenska, born on 30 September 1947 and married to 'Minder' star Dennis Waterman.

My amazing fact _____

_____

_____

October

October 1

First there were British chips, then there were
French fries, and then there were . . . Red Indian
potato crisps! Their inventor's name was George
Crum, which doesn't sound very Red Indian
to me!

My amazing fact _____

_____

_____

WELL, YOU
LEARN SOMETHING
EVERY DAY,
DON'T YOU...

October 2

Amazing Animals
Just imagine, a cow's 'moo' was used to measure
distance in India for over 2000 years.

My amazing fact _____

_____

_____

October 3

In Cuba many people believe that walking bare
headed in the moonlight is dangerous and never
do it.

My amazing fact _____

_____

_____

October 4

Until 1970, parents in France had to choose first
names for their children from a list published by
the government.

My amazing fact _____

_____

_____

October 5

The town of Scunthorpe was named after a
Danish pirate with a squint.

My amazing fact _____

_____

_____

October 6

On 6 October 1965 the Post Office Tower opened in London — at 620 ft (188.9km) it was then the tallest building in London. Sadly it had to be closed to the public in 1971 for security reasons.

My amazing fact _____

_____

_____

October 7

Medical Madness
Zzz-zzz — man is the only animal that sleeps on his back, and just as amazing is the fact that horses can sleep standing up!

My amazing fact _____

_____

_____

October 8

Frightening Phobia
Agoraphobics hate deserts. They have a fear of open spaces, and sufferers don't even go out of doors.

My amazing fact _____

_____

_____

October 9

If a camel is nicknamed 'the ship of the desert' because it can 'sail' for so long without water, what should we call rats? They can survive without water even longer than camels can.

My amazing fact _____

_____

_____

October 10

As a Matter of Fact
More films are made in India than in Hollywood, or France, or Italy. In 1984 a total of 833 different films were made in the various Indian languages.

My amazing fact _____

_____

_____

October 11

Beanz Meanz Heinz!
There really was a Mr H. J. Heinz, who founded the Heinz food company which now makes many more than 57 varieties. Baked beans were always Mr Heinz's favourites.

My amazing fact _____

_____

_____

October 12

Bodily Business

By the time you've read to the end of this sentence, 50,000,000 of your body's cells will have died and been replaced; all except for your brain cells that is — they're never replaced!

My amazing fact _____

_____

_____

October 13

Today some men go to the barber for a 'short back and sides'; in the Victorian era it was a 'shave and a haircut'; in the Middle Ages it was a '*bath* and a haircut'!

My amazing fact _____

_____

_____

October 14

The battle of Hastings was fought today. Of course you always knew it happened in 1066 — but now you know it happened on 14 October.

My amazing fact _____

_____

_____

October 15

Happy Birthday to . . .
Her Royal Highness The Duchess of York — still 'Fergie' to her friends — who was born on this day in 1959.

My amazing fact _____

_____

_____

October 16

The playwright Oscar Wilde was born on this day in 1854. His full name was Oscar Fingal O'Flahertie Wills Wilde, and he was born in Dublin.

My amazing fact _____

_____

_____

October 17

Geographical Gem
The island of Pitcairn, in the Pacific Ocean, is the smallest state in the world, and has a population of just 100 people.

My amazing fact _____

_____

_____

October 18

Ridiculous but Real
Horses were originally native to the Americas, but died out there about 10,000 years ago. 100 years after Christopher Columbus 'discovered' America, the Spaniards reintroduced horses.

My amazing fact _____

_____

_____

October 19

The saying goes that on a clear day you can see forever. And you could also say that on a clear day — if you're in the Arctic — you can hear forever. Well, you can hear people talking over 1 ¾ miles (3km) away.

My amazing fact _____

_____

_____

October 20

In Britain some people believe we have too few public holidays. Perhaps the government could think of declaring half-day public holidays , which happen in some countries, like Brazil and Iceland.

My amazing fact _____

_____

_____

October 21

October is the month for famous battles. It was on 21 October 1805 that Admiral Lord Nelson signalled the start of the Battle of Trafalgar, and others fought this month include the Battle of El Alamein on 23 October 1942, and on 25 October both the Battle of Agincourt (1415) and the Battle of Balaclava (1854), famous for the Charge of the Light Brigade.

My amazing fact _____

_____

_____

October 22

Food Fact
Fully-grown whales eat about 3 tons of food each day. They feed off minute animals and plants

called plankton, and take in huge amounts of
water with the plankton, sift out the food and
shoot the water out through their blowholes.

My amazing fact _____

_____

_____

October 23

October Odyssey
It would take you 4000 years to name all the stars
in the Milky Way if you managed to say one name
every second. You start naming if you want to —
I'm not going to!

My amazing fact _____

_____

_____

October 24

War and Peace
For every year of peace there have been ten years
of war in the history of the world.

My amazing fact _____

_____

_____

October 25

As a Matter of Fact
The official title for the country of Uruguay is the Oriental Republic of Uruguay. Well, it is on the eastern side of south America, and oriental does mean 'eastern'.

My amazing fact _____

_____

_____

October 26

Sporting Success
And happy birthday to the Football Association, which was 'born' on 26 October 1863. Their original goal was to 'prevent vicious tactical fouls' — something they're still aiming for!

My amazing fact _____

_____

_____

October 27

'Break a leg' is the theatrical way of saying 'Good Luck' because it's supposed to be bad luck to say 'Good Luck'! Another theatrical superstition is that fresh flowers must never be used on stage.

My amazing fact _____

_____

_____

October 28

Queen Victoria was the first monarch to have a state funeral. Up until her reign members of the royal family were buried secretly at night.

My amazing fact _____

_____

_____

October 29

Fun Fact of the Month
This comes a bit early this month so as not to upset the vampires, witches, and ghosts who will be out and about on Hallowe'en. Do you know that it costs 24 pounds to collect and process a pint of blood from a donor? (Vampires don't pay, though, they get their blood free!)

My amazing fact _____

_____

_____

October 30

There are supposed to be more ghosts per square km in England than any other country in the world.

My amazing fact _____

_____

_____

October 31

Hallowe'en has been observed for centuries, and people used to believe that they had to dress like ghosts so they would be mistaken for fellow-spirits — and left unharmed!

My amazing fact _____

_____

_____

WELL I NEVER!

November

November 1

The first-ever escalator in Britain was installed at Harrods in 1898. The nervous passengers had to be revived at the end of their journey with smelling salts!

My amazing fact _____

_____

_____

November 2

Sporting Success
An American golfer called Floyd S. Reed set out to drive golf balls across the width of America — and succeeded! The distance was 3500 miles (5632.5km) and it is estimated that he lost the same number of golf balls during his marathon.

My amazing fact _____

_____

_____

November 3

There is a plant called the 'Sensitive Plant' (or 'Shame Lady') in the Caribbean that folds its leaves when you touch it — as if it really were sensitive or shy!

My amazing fact _____

_____

_____

November 4

Pound for Pound — Kilo for Kilo
2590 pounds (1174.8kg) of extra fuel is needed aboard for every extra pound (just under half a kilogram) of weight carried on a space flight. Of course, astronauts aren't allowed to be overweight.

My amazing fact _____

_____

_____

November 5

Today is Guy Fawkes' Day, named after the man who tried to blow up the Houses of Parliament in 1607.

My amazing fact _____

_____

_____

November 6

Why are lots of clowns called Joey!
   They're named after Joseph (Joey) Grimaldi, the most famous clown of his day.

My amazing fact _____

_____

_____

November 7

November Naughtiness

Some say a man called Thomas Crapper invented the loo — he certainly was a loo salesman — but in fact a flush toilet has been discovered at a palace in Knossos, Crete, dating from 2000 BC.

My amazing fact _____

_____

_____

November 8

The biggest fish and chip shop in the world was opened by Harry Ramsden in Guiseley, Yorkshire, in 1931. Nearly 200 tons of fish is fried there each year.

My amazing fact _____

_____

_____

November 9

Geographical Gem
The Amazon River, which winds through South America, has more water in it than the total amount of water in the *eight* next largest rivers.

My amazing fact _____

_____

_____

November 10

Why do Eskimo children eat whale meat and blubber?
   You'd blubber too at the thought of the 120 barrels of oil that come from the blubber of just one blue whale.

My amazing fact _____

_____

_____

November 11

Medical thermometers were originally so large it took five minutes to take someone's temperature. Nowadays temperatures can be taken in seconds and the thermometers are digital.

My amazing fact _____

_____

_____

November 12

Happy Birthday to . . .
Jillean Hipsey, captain of the England netball
team and the most capped player ever. She has
won a total of 84 caps.

My amazing fact _____
_____
_____

November 13

As a Matter of Fact . . .
The baker's dozen used to be a form of bakers'
insurance: heavy fines were imposed on bakers
who short-changed their customers, so for every
12 loaves bought, the baker would throw in an
extra one to be on the safe side.

My amazing fact _____
_____
_____

November 14

Happy Birthday to . . .
His Royal Highness The Prince of Wales, born on
14 November 1948 and christened Charles Philip
Arthur George. He was invested as the Prince of
Wales in 1969.

My amazing fact _____
_____
_____

November 15

Medical Madness

Do you take cod liver oil to keep you healthy in winter?

Surprisingly this medicine contains vitamins obtained from the sun — but the cod fish never sees the sun!

My amazing fact _____

_____

_____

November 16

It's a fact that more people eat vanilla-flavoured ice cream than any other flavour.

My amazing fact _____

_____

_____

November 17

Amazing Animals

How do snakes hear, when they don't appear to have ears?

Easy: they hear through their tongues, by receiving sound waves.

My amazing fact _____

_____

_____

November 18

Bodily Business
Humans hear when sound waves are gathered
into the inner ear, making the fluid in it vibrate.
Electrical messages are then carried to the brain
for decoding.

My amazing fact _____

_____

_____

November 19

Wouldn't it be wonderful to watch the sun rise
over the Pacific Ocean and watch it set over the
Atlantic Ocean?

   You could — if you were at the Panama Canal,
because of the curve in the land through which the
Canal was carved out.

My amazing fact _____

_____

_____

November 20

Have you ever noticed how seagulls flock inland
during bad weather?

   They're searching for food. They won't get fish,

of course, but like any other birds they're looking for worms which surface after rain.

My amazing fact _____

_____

_____

November 21

Caution — Hard Hat Area
We know how important hard hats are, on building sites and down coal mines, but did you know that they were first worn over 400 years ago by the men who built the Vatican?

My amazing fact _____

_____

_____

November 22

Ridiculous but Real
There is a piece of music called 'Imaginary Landscape No 4' which was 'written' by composer John Cage — for twelve randomly-tuned radios!

My amazing fact _____

_____

_____

November 23

Parliament in Iceland is called the 'Althing' and is the oldest in the world. Established in 930, it has governed since then without interruption.

My amazing fact _____

_____

_____

November 24

Silly bears, they've been climbing telegraph poles in search of honey. They do it because they mistake the humming in the wires for bees in the hive.

My amazing fact _____

_____

_____

November 25

The world's longest-running show opened on this day in 1952. Agatha Christie's 'The Mousetrap' has had over 14,500 performances and been seen by more than seven million people.

My amazing fact _____

_____

_____

November 26

Food Fact
Edward III, who reigned in the 14th century, passed a law making it illegal for his subjects to eat more than twice a day, and in fact it was 500 years later that people living in the Western world began to eat three meals a day.

My amazing fact _____

_____

_____

November 27

There are so many books being added to the famous Yale University Library in the United States that it's been estimated that by the year 2000 the volumes could reach from the equator to the North Pole. (If we sent the Amazing Fact-a-

Day Fun Book, do you think that would help them
reach their target on 31 December 1999?)

My amazing fact _____

_____

_____

November 28

Hot or Cold
Warm water freezes more quickly than cold
water, and boiling water is cooler than is water
just before it boils. Incredible but it's a fact.

My amazing fact _____

_____

_____

November 29

This fun fact is printed in a typeface called 'Italic', which was invented in 1500.

My amazing fact _____

_____

_____

November 30

Fun Fact of the Month
Why is a Boeing 747 jet aeroplane nicknamed the Jumbo Jet?
    Because it weighs as much as 67 elephants — over 380 tons!

My amazing fact _____

_____

_____

December

December 1

BOO to the English Parliament which abolished Christmas in 1647.

My amazing fact _____

_____

_____

December 2

HOORAY to the reign of Charles II, which began in 1660, for restoring Christmas!

My amazing fact _____

_____

_____

December 3

In South Africa on 3 December 1967 Dr Christian Barnard performed the first ever heart transplant operation. Everybody said it couldn't be done, but look what a long way transplant surgery has come since then!

My amazing fact _____

_____

_____

December 4

Charles Darrow invented the game of Monopoly on 4 December 1935. Today, over 500 million games have been sold.

My amazing fact _____

_____

_____

December 5

Walt Disney was born today in 1901. And guess whose was the original Micky Mouse voice! Walt Disney's of course!

My amazing fact _____

_____

_____

December 6

Today is the Feast Day of St Nicholas, who is also the patron saint of sailors and schoolboys, beermakers and dockers!

My amazing fact _____

_____

_____

December 7

The British royal family exchange their Christmas presents on Christmas Eve.

My amazing fact _____

_____

_____

December 8

The most popular Christmas song ever recorded is 'White Christmas'. It was first published in the summer of 1942. 'Away in a Manger' was published in the summer too, so we've always shopped early for Christmas.

My amazing fact _____

_____

_____

December 9

The ITV programme, 'Coronation Street', started on 9 December, 1960. Believe it or not, it was only supposed to run for six weeks — soon it will be celebrating its 30th _year_.

My amazing fact _____

_____

_____

December 10

Do you like watching snow?

I do, for about five minutes — and then I go cross eyed trying to watch *each* snowflake to see if they really are all different. Scientists say they are, but I find it really hard to believe that of all the millions, billions, trillions of snowflakes that have fallen (and that's just in my lifetime!) no two have been alike.

My amazing fact _____

_____

_____

December 11

On 11th December 1936, Edward VIII gave up the British throne — for the love of Mrs Wallis Simpson.

My amazing fact _____

_____

_____

December 12

Ridiculous but Real
You may be dreaming of a white Christmas, but if you live in London you're unlikely to get one. In London snow has fallen on Christmas Day only once since the start of the century.

My amazing fact _____

_____

_____

December 13

As a Matter of Fact
Women used to tie holly to their bedsteads so that they didn't become witches. I _hope_ they picked the holly from the topmost branches of the tree where it's least prickly!

My amazing fact _____

_____

_____

December 14

Cellophane paper was once so expensive that it was used to wrap only the most expensive presents.

My amazing fact _____

_____

_____

December 15

December Datum
Christmas is a widely observed holiday, on which neither the past nor the future is of as much interest as . . . the present!

My amazing fact _____

_____

_____

December 16

The Boston Tea Party was held today in 1773 in the USA. But it wasn't a jolly affair — it was in fact a protest raid on the tea clippers (ships) waiting in Boston harbour to unload their cargo. The 'tea rebels' boarded the clippers and threw over 300 tea chests into the harbour — only to discover that the tide was out!

My amazing fact _____

_____

_____

December 17

Have you put a kaleidoscope on your Christmas list this year?

You might not know it, but kaleidoscopes were originally invented to help designers of cloth to make up new patterns.

My amazing fact _____

_____

_____

December 18

Happy Birthday to . . .
Steven Spielberg, born on 18 December 1947. He is, of course, the 'boy who never grew up' of the film world, and the maker of 'ET' and 'American Tail'.

My amazing fact _____

_____

_____

December 19

Amazing Animals
A grasshopper's legs can walk on their own! Even if they're detached from the insect, they'll keep stepping out. . . .

My amazing fact _____

_____

_____

December 20

Happy Birthday to . . .
Jenny Agutter, born on 20 December 1952. She
was the child star of 'The Railway Children'.

My amazing fact _____

_____

_____

December 21

Medical Madness
If you eat one tomato, it gives you one calorie of
energy — just enough to read about 650 words!

My amazing fact _____

_____

_____

December 22

Sporting Success
This month, the sporting success is anyone who
goes for a Christmas swim or braves the sea on
Boxing Day — and lots of people do! Sometimes
they have to break the ice on a lake to take their
dip, or shiver off a pier in the icy sea, but they say
it's tradition!

My amazing fact _____

_____

_____

December 23

Differences in Common
What do you think the giraffe, the cat and the camel have in common?

You might be able to tell if you watched closely as they walk — they move both left legs together, and then both right legs, other animals have 'cross-pattern' walking.

My amazing fact _____

_____

_____

December 24

'Twas the night before Christmas, when all through the house — the tension was mounting!' The Scottish poet William McGonagall used to write poetry as badly as that — some people call him the worst poet the world has ever known!

My amazing fact _____

_____

_____

WELL I NEVER!

December 25

Christmas Day!
25 December was first celebrated as the date of the birth of Jesus in 440, and a Happy Christmas birthday to Her Royal Highness Princess Alexandra, who was born in 1936, and to Kenny Everett, who was born in 1944.

My amazing fact _____

_____

_____

December 26

Boxing day is so called not because of boxing fights, but because, once upon a time, earthenware collecting boxes were opened and given to the poor.

My amazing fact _____

_____

_____

December 27

What was Gatwick Airport before it was Gatwick Airport?
  A goat farm!

My amazing fact _____

_____

_____

December 28

'Acronym' is the term given to a word which is made up of the first letters of other words. 'Posh' is an acronym. It is used to describe a way to travel to India by liner — Port Out, Starboard Home — during which the cabin would be away from the sun.

My amazing fact _____

_____

_____

December 29

Food Fact
Probably your Christmas pudding is all eaten up. But did you know that the traditional plum pudding recipe probably originated in Germany, and was brought to this country by Prince Albert, husband of Queen Victoria?

My amazing fact _____

_____

_____

December 30

Bodily Business

As the year draws to a close, you might like to know that the adult heart beats about 70 times in one minute — that's 36,792,000 times a year. But as you're not *quite* an adult, yours has probably done a little less work this year.

My amazing fact _____

_____

_____

December 31

It's New Year's Eve . . . or Old Year's Night . . . or Hogmanay. The last is a very Scottish celebration for seeing in the new year, but the word 'Hogmanay' most probably comes from the Norman French word, 'Aguillanneuf'. Happy New Year!

My amazing fact _____

_____

_____